My name is Alberto Barambio Canet, a passionate traveler who creates travel content under the name '1 Hour Travel Guides'. In 2021, I set myself the goal of sharing my travel experiences and showing the world that there is another life beyond working 9-5.

In 2019 I started living in Ho Chi Minh City, Vietnam, working as a math teacher in an international school. Teaching in schools abroad has allowed me to travel to places I never imagined and to get to know the culture and peo-

forced me to stay in Vietnam for my summer vacation since the country's borders were closed. So I traveled through Vietnam from north to south.

With this e-book I intend:

1. To be able to share my knowledge about the destination of Vietnam and the culture.

2. That you don't go crazy searching for information on thousands of blogs on the Internet. This guide will provide you a great starting point and summary of the routes, transportation, and basics to start your trip.

3. To provide inspiration and visual references to know what to expect on your trip to Vietnam.

# 1 HOUR TRAVEL GUIDES

✉ ABARAMBIO1@GMAIL.COM

ⓕ 1 HOUR TRAVEL GUIDES

⧄ @1HOURTRAVELGUIDES

✦ LINKTR.EE/1HOURTRAVELGUIDES

GOLDEN BRIDGE

# INDEX

CAVES IN PHONG NHA

# Introduction

All **recommendations** and advice in this book come from my **own research** and **experiences** traveling in **Vietnam**.

Although I have written the book with the best of care, I don't guarantee that the content is completely free from minor errors. Therefore, 'Viaja, son dos días' may contain erroneous or outdated information.

Copyright on the writing and illustrations in this guide. Nothing may be copied, changed or distributed without permission of the author.

# Before your trip

INFO ABOUT VIETNAM | WEATHER AND BEST
TIME TO GO | TRAVEL PREPARATIONS | HOW TO
PACK

Ha Giang

Sapa

Halong

HANOI

Ninh Binh

Phong Nha

# Vietnam

Hue

Danang

Hoian

HO CHI MINH

Phu Quoc

# ¿Did you know...?

*The average height* of the Vietnamese is *159cm.*

*There are 47 million motorcycles* in Vietnam and only **2 million cars.**

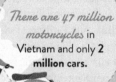

*Vietnam is the second largest exporter of coffee beans.*

**People want** to have the **whitest skin** possible. You'll see skin-whitening products, people covering themselves from head to toe even in 40-degree heat, and beaches that are empty except at sunrise or sunset.

*The Vietnamese new year*

is celebrated every year on a different date **between** the months of **January** and **February,** coinciding with the Chinese New Year.

Vietnam's capital is **Hanoi:** *Vietnam has a population of 97.4 million people.*

# Weather
## *and best time to go*

### BEST TIME
There is **no ideal time** to visit Vietnam because it has more than **2,000 km** of **coastline** and **3 different climates**. Anyway, if you plan to tour the country from north to south, the best months are from September to December, March and April.

### MONSOON SEASON

### SOUTHWEST OF THE COUNTRY
May to September.

### NORTHWEST VIETNAM
November to March.

### THE WEATHER CAN BE DIVIDED INTO 3 REGIONS

### HANOI AND THE NORTH
**May through October** is very **hot** and humid with huge **rainfalls**. From November to April there is no rain, but it can be cold. Further **north** from Hanoi, from **December to January** it can be **very cold** as they are regions at higher altitudes and surrounded by mountains.

### CENTRAL VIETNAM
Hot and dry from January to August with temperatures around 30 degrees. The **rainy season** is between **September, October and November**.

### SOUTH VIETNAM AND SAIGON
Warm and without rainfall between the months of November to April; the **rainy season** runs from **May to October**.

**BEACH IN PHU QUOC**

### *Tip*
My advice is the following: travel to Vietnam when you are on vacation regardless of the calendar. If you intend to travel from north to south, you will never find a time with perfect weather.

| Destinations | JAN | FEB | MAR | APR | MAY | JUN | JUL | AUG | SEP | OCT | NOV | DEC |
|---|---|---|---|---|---|---|---|---|---|---|---|---|
| Sapa | | | | | | | | | | | | |
| Ha Giang | | | | | | | | | | | | |
| Hanoi | | | | | | | | | | | | |
| Halong Bay | | | | | | | | | | | | |
| Ninh Binh | | | | | | | | | | | | |
| Phong Nha | | | | | | | | | | | | |
| Hue | | | | | | | | | | | | |
| Danang | | | | | | | | | | | | |
| Hoian | | | | | | | | | | | | |
| Saigon | | | | | | | | | | | | |
| Mekong | | | | | | | | | | | | |
| Phu Quoc | | | | | | | | | | | | |

Best time   Ok   Worst time   North Vietnam   Central Vietnam   South Vietnam

11

# Travel
*preparations*

## PLANE TICKETS

This is usually the **general rule** for buying plane tickets: **Buying early** will **save** you **money**. You can find the cheapest flights at **www.momondo.com** or **www.skyscanner.com**

These flight search engines allow you to track the best prices for weeks and send you alerts when they are cheaper.

## VISA

There is a list of 24 countries that don't need a visa to enter Vietnam. If you are not so lucky that your country is on this list, there are **2 ways** to **get** a **visa** to travel to Vietnam: **online** (ETA) and upon arrival at Hanoi or Ho Chi Minh **airport**.

### ETA (ELECTRONIC TRAVEL AUTHORISATION O ONLINE VISA)

**Getting** a **visa** for Vietnam **online** is very **easy** and can be done online. Although the process takes about **3 days,** don't wait until the last minute to do it. Its cost is:

* $25 valid for **30 days** (**single entry**).

* $50 for **3 months** (**multi-entry**).

*Tip*
The rules to enter Vietnam may have changed due to Covid requirements. Check this link for the latest news: borderless.safetywing.com

### VISA ON ARRIVAL FROM VIETNAM

The most comfortable option is to process the visa when you arrive at the **Ho Chi Minh** or **Hanoi airport**. **Don't forget** to bring **2 passport size photos** (4x6 cm) and **25/50 dollars** in **cash** to pay the visa costs.

# Travel *preparations*

- *Grab*

Traveling in Vietnam can be ridiculously cheap. **Grab** is the app used by locals and expats in Vietnam to get around by **taxi**. The app allows you to request a trip by **motorcycle or car**. I recommend the motorcycle option, in addition to being a unique experience, traveling about 6 km can cost you as little as $1.50. You can also order food at home with this app.

- *Google Maps*

Very useful to be able to move about easily in your destinations. **Download** Vietnam **maps** to use in **offline** locations.

- *XE currency*

To know the **conversion** of the **Vietnamese Dong to your** own **currency**.

- *Google translator*

App to **translate languages**. Very useful to avoid misunderstandings and to be able to communicate even if you are in a remote village in Vietnam.

- *Splitwise*

Great app if you **travel** in a **group**. It helps to **keep track** of **costs** of the trip and **split expenses**.

Vietnam is a country that is adapted to tourism and you can find Wi-Fi connection in practically **all restaurants, cafes** and **accommodations**.

## SIMCARD

Buy a SIM card as soon as you arrive at the airport. Before leaving the terminal there are points of sale where they can sell you a chip. I recommend the Viettel. It is the provider that most people use. It has coverage in almost the entire country and is the most reliable company.

## DATA PLANS

In Vietnam data plans are cheap. For example, a 10GB data package valid for one month costs about 5 dollars. Or the 20 GB package, about $8.80.

# Travel *preparations*

## TRAVEL INSURANCE

Although **traveling** in **Vietnam** is **safe**, we **must be prepared** in case we have a medical **emergency**, have to cancel our trip or our belongings are stolen.

The insurance I use on my trips is "Safetywing". Check it out to travel without worries. Insurance **covers up to $250,000** in emergencies and **costs** around **$21 for 2 weeks** of travel.

## VACCINES

As of today, the Covid vaccine is mandatory to enter Vietnam. In addition, the following vaccinations are recommended (for safety, check the list of vaccinations with your doctor):

- Hepatitis A
- Hepatitis B
- Typhoid fever
- Encefalítis japonesa
- Japanese encephalitis
- Rabies
- Diphtheria

In any case, don't forget to **use** mosquito **repellent**. **There is dengue, zika, malaria** (even in big cities) and there is no effective vaccine to protect you.

## BASIC HYGIENE RECOMMENDATIONS

- **Don't drink tap water** and **avoid** drinking **iced drinks** from **street** stalls.
- Wash your hands and bring **antibacterial gel**.
- Travel with **diarrhea tablets** as it is common for tourists to get stomach ailments during the trip.

# Travel *preparations*

## BACKPACK OR SUITCASE?

Depending on your traveling style and route you can choose either of the two. Traveling with a **backpack** is **more practical** and you may find it more comfortable if you go to more **rural areas** or travel by train or **motorcycle**. However, many people still travel with a suitcase, which can save you from back pain.

## * DON'T FORGET:

• That your **passport** is **valid** for at least **6 months**.
• Get **vaccinated** at least **4 weeks before** your trip.
• Organize and store all the documents for your trip in an easily accessible place.
• Request your **visa a few weeks before** the trip.
• **Download** and **test** the **apps** before leaving.
• **Carry this book** on your trip.

## WHAT TO PUT IN YOUR SUITCASE?

**Packing** for **Vietnam** is **no easy** task. As there are **3 different climatic zones** throughout the country, you can experience very different situations:

• If you are going to the **north** of the country, you'll probably need **warm clothes**.
• It is also **very likely** that in some **parts** of your **trip** it is **rainy season** and you will need a **raincoat**.
• Something that you will **not** be able to **avoid** in any of the destination is **hot** conditions and high humidity.
• I advise you not to bring too many clothes. **Most hotels** and hostels offer **laundry services** at very affordable prices.

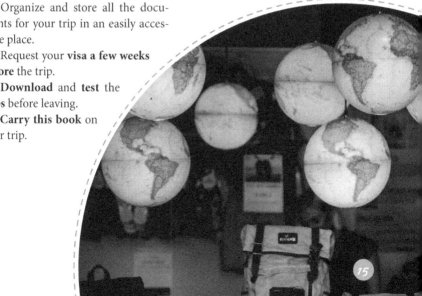

# List

## DOCUMENTS

- Passport
- Wallet
- Credit card
- Travel insurance
- Copy of important documents
- Passport size photos for the visa
- International driver's license

## TRAVEL ESSENTIALS

- Backpack or suitcase
- Day trip backpack
- Microfiber towel
- Flip flops
- Walking shoes
- Universal adapter
- Padlock

## ELECTRONIC PRODUCTS

- Camera and memory cards
- Power bank
- Phone
- Chargers

## CLOTHING

- Raincoat
- Sweatshirt
- Jacket
- Sweatshirt
- 1 long-sleeved T-shirt
- Shorts
- Short sleeve t-shirts
- Underwear
- 1 dress/skirt
- 1 sarong
- Sunglasses
- Belt

## PERSONAL CARE PRODUCTS

- Sunscreen
- Mosquito repellent
- Antibacterial gel
- Deodorant
- Toothbrush and toothpaste
- Razor
- Feminine hygiene products
- Hair brush
- Paracetamol
- Diarrhea tablets

FANSIPAN

*Itineraries*

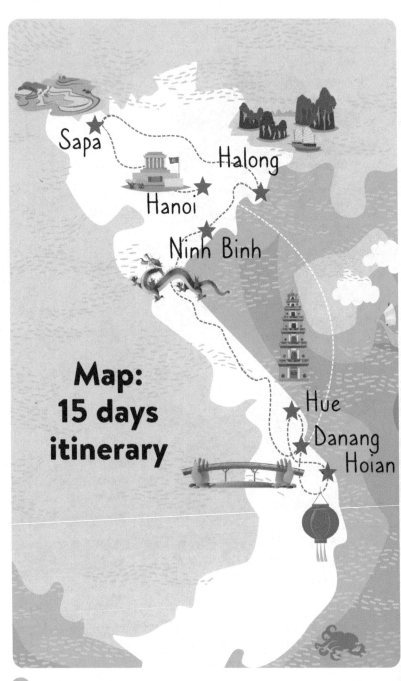

Sapa

Halong

Hanoi

Ninh Binh

**Map:
15 days
itinerary**

Hue

Danang

Hoian

# 15 days itinerary
## (7 destinations)

Before talking about the route, you should know the most **common options** to **enter Vietnam**:

• International **Airport** Noi Bai (**Hanoi**, north of the country)
• International **Airport** Tan Son Nhat (**Ho Chi Minh City,** south)

In order not to get confused when you arrive in the country, it is worth knowing that the **Vietnamese names** of **most cities** are written in **two syllables.** You can **read it** in just **1 word to simplify it.** Here are some examples:

• **Hà Nội**- Hanoi
• **Hội An**- Hoian
• **Đà Nẵng**- Danang

There are **3 key destinations** on your trip: **Hanoi (north), Danang (center) and Ho Chi Minh City (south).** They will be your stops from where you can travel to other parts of the country since they usually have more accommodation and transportation options.

Although my **suggested route** is from **north to south**, you can **also do the trip** in the **opposite direction**.

LITERATURE
TEMPLE- HANOI

**DAY 1-2** HANOI

Hanoi is the **capital** of Vietnam, located in the **north** of Vietnam. It can be your stop at the **beginning** of your **trip** since it is relatively **close** to several recommended destinations: **Sapa, Halong Bay** and **Ninh Binh.**

Upon arrival, get used to the chaos of the city center and contrast with the Vietnamese culture. Enjoy its **temples**, **architecture**, the chaotic city center and dare to eat **street food**.

# 15 days itinerary
## (7 destinations)

### DAY 3-5 SAPA

Take the **train** or **night bus** to **save time** (6-7 hours away).

Stay with an ethnic family (**homestay**) for a unique experience.

Enjoy its **wonderful landscapes** and don't forget to **bring warm clothes** as it can be cold in this mountainous area.

LANDSCAPES IN SAPA

Transportation from
HANOI TO SAPA

🚌 BUS | 6H | $12
   *Recommended*

🚆 TRAIN | 9H | $19
   LUXURY TRAIN | 9H | $27

🚕 TAXI: 5.5H, $170

🚐 VAN: 5.5 H, $18

### DÍA 6-7 HALONG BAY

Just **2 hours from** the **capital** you can visit one of the **heritage sites** of Vietnam: Halong Bay. Don't miss the opportunity to take a **cruise** to view the beautiful **hills scattered** by the sea, relax on one of its beaches or practice kayaking. I recommend that you spend only one day at this destination so that you have time to visit the rest of the destinations.

Transportation from
SAPA TO BAHÍA HALONG BAY

🚌 BUS | 8 H, $19
   *Recommended*

🚕 TAXI: 7.5 H, $232

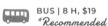

HALONG BAY

# 15 days *(7 destinations)*

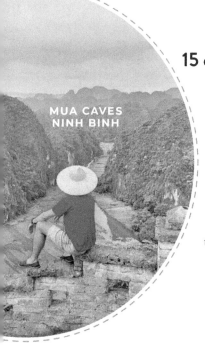

**MUA CAVES NINH BINH**

Go from Halong Bay to reach Ninh Binh, one of my favorite destinations in Vietnam. The city offers **landscapes** worthy of a National Geographic documentary. The views from the top of "Mua Caves" and a **boat ride** through Tam Coc will be some of your best memories on the trip to Vietnam.

Transporation from
HA LONG TO NINH BINH

 VAN: 3.5 H, $14
*Recommended*

 BUS | 5H | $7
TAXI: 3.5H, $78

**DAY 10-11** DANANG

**Take a flight** to reach Danang. This will be your second stop of the trip since from this destination you can **easily travel to** the cities of **Hue** and **Hoian**. In addition, you can visit the '**Golden Bridge**' in this city, and enjoy some of the best beaches in the country.

From DANANG TO HUE

 BUS | 3H | $7
*Recommended*

 TREIN | 2.5H | $6

 TAXI: 2.5H, $56

 VAN: 2 H, $56

**KHAI DINH TUMBS, HUE**

# 15 days *(7 destinations)*

## DAY 12  HUE

Just over **2 hours north of Danang**, you can visit one of the **most historical cities** in Vietnam. Marvel at the **Imperial City** and the **tombs of ancient emperors**. Hue was the capital of Vietnam for 150 years (in the 19th and 20th centuries).

Transportation from
HANOI TO DANANG

 BUS | 15H | $16

 TAXI: 15.5H, $32.9

PLANE: 1.20 H, $23
*Recommended option*

IMPERIAL CITY-HUE

## DAY 13-14  HOIAN

Just **45 minutes from Danang** is the most charming city in the country. Here you can take a Vietnamese **cooking class**, tour its **beautiful historic center**, enjoy the hundreds of **colored lanterns** that illuminate Hoian, or relax on its **beaches**.

Transportation from
HUE TO HOIAN

 BUS | 4H | $7

 TAXI: 2.45H, $56

 VAN: 3H, $16
*Recommended option*

OLD TOWN-HOIAN

# 15 days *(7 destinations)*

**DAY 15**  HANOI

Take advantage of your **last day** in the capital to **buy souvenirs** of your trip to Vietnam. To **return to Hanoi**, you have to take a **flight** from Da-nang City.

Transportation from
HOIAN TO DANANG

 BUS | 1.5H | $6

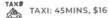 TAXI: 45MINS, $16

 VAN: 50MINS, $7
*Recommended option*

Transportation from
DANANG TO HANOI

✈ PLANE| 1H20MIN | $35

TRAN QUOC
PAGODA-HANOI

23

Map:
1 month
itinerary

# 1 month itinerary
## *(11 destinations)*

### DAY 1-2 HANOI

Hanoi is the **capital** of **Vietnam**, located in the **north** of Vietnam. It can be your stop at the beginning of your trip since it is relatively **close to** several recommended destinations: **Sapa, Halong Bay, Ha Giang** and **Ninh Binh**.

Upon arrival, get used to the chaos of the city center and contrast with the Vietnamese culture.

### DAY 3-5 SAPA

Take the **train or night bus** to save time and hotel nights (**6-7 hours away**).

Stay with an ethnic family (**homestay**) for a unique experience .

Enjoy its wonderful **landscapes** and don't forget to bring **warm clothes** as it can be cold in this **mountainous area.**

Transportation from
HANOI TO SAPA

BUS | 6H | $12
*Recommended*

TRAIN | 9H | $19
LUXURY TRAIN | 9H | $27

TAXI: 5.5H, $170

VAN: 5.5 H, $18

### DAY 6-9 HA GIANG LOOP

Continue your journey through the **spectacular landscapes** of **northern Vietnam**. **Rent** a **motorcycle** and enjoy **zig-zag roads between mountain** canyons. You will get to know **areas** where time seems to have stopped and where they have **barely seen foreigners**. It is one of the newest tourist destinations in Vietnam.

Transportation from
SAPA TO HA GIANG

VAN | 6H, $17
*Recommended option*

TAXI: 6H, $165

HA GIANG LOOP
STARTING POINT

# 1 month itinerary
## *(11 destinations)*

**DAY 10-11**  HANOI

After a long trip discovering the wonders of northern Vietnam, **take some time** to casually get to **know** the country's **capital**. Enjoy its **temples**, **architecture** and dare to eat the delicious Vietnamese **street food**.

STREETS IN HANOI

Transportion from
HA GIANG TO HANOI

 VAN: 6H, $17
*Recommended*

 BUS | 6H | $1

**DAY 12-13**  HALONG BAY

Just **2 hours from the capital** you can visit one of the **heritage sites** of tourism in Vietnam: Halong Bay. Don't miss the opportunity to take a **cruise** to see the beautiful **hills scattered** by the sea, relax on one of its **beaches** or **visit** its **largest island, Cat Ba**.

Transportation from
HANOI TO HALONG BAY

 BUS: 2-3 H, $7
*Recommended*

 VAN: 2.5-3.5H, $13

 TAXI: 2-3H, $15

 TRAIN: 7H, $6

 PLANE: 45 MIN, $185

HALONG BAY

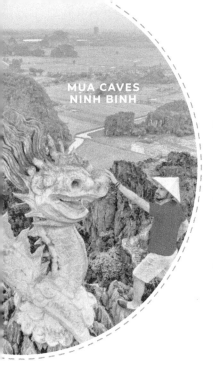

MUA CAVES
NINH BINH

# 1 month itinerary
## *(11 destinations)*

**DAY 14-15** NINH BINH

Move from Halong Bay to reach Ninh Binh, one of my favorite destinations in Vietnam. The city offers **landscapes** worthy of a National Geographic documentary. Its views from the top of "Mua Caves" and its **boat ride** through Tam Coc will be some of your best memories on the trip to Vietnam.

Transportation from
HA LONG TO NINH BINH

 VAN: 3.5 H. $14
*\*Recommended option*

 BUS: 5H, $7
 TAXI: 3.5 H, $78

**DAY 16-18** PHONG NHA

Continue your way south to reach the **center of Vietnam**. Phong Nha is still a little known destination internationally. There you can find movie **landscapes**, go on an **adventure** in the **jungle** and explore the **largest caves** in the **world**. Although it is not as well connected as other destinations, you can get there after a few hours by bus or plane.

Transportation from
NINH BINH-PHONG NHA

 TRAIN: 9 H, $20
*\*Recommended*

 BUS: 8H, $13
 TAXI: 7H, $191

PHONG NHA
CAVES

# 1 month itinerary
## *(11 destinations)*

**DAY 19**  HUE

One of the most **historic cities** in Vietnam. Marvel at the **Imperial City** and the **tombs** of **ancient emperors**. Hue was for 150 years (in the 19th and 20th centuries) the capital of Vietnam.

Transportation from
PHONG NHA TO HUE

 **BUS: 4 H, $7**
*Recommended*

 TAXI: 4 H, $88

 TRAIN: 3H, $12

**DAY 20-22**  DANANG

I recommend that you travel by **train from Hue** for its **wonderful views** of the **sea**. In this destination you can visit the '**Golden Bridge**' and enjoy some of the **best beaches** in the country.

Transportation from
HUE TO DANANG

 TRAIN: 2.5 H, $9
*Recommended*

 BUS: 3H, $7

 TAXI: 2.5 H, $59

 VAN: 2 H, $10

DRAGON BRIDGE
DANANG

✈ PLANE: 45 MIN, $185

# 1 month *(11 destinations)*

## DAY 23-24  HOIAN

Just **45 minutes from Danang** is the most charming city in the country. Here you can take a Vietnamese **cooking class**, tour its **beautiful historic center**, enjoy the hundreds of **colored lanterns** that illuminate Hoian at night, or relax on its **beaches**.

Transportation from
DANANG TO HOIAN

 VAN: 50 MIN, $7
*Recommended option*

 BUS: 1.5 H, $6
 TAXI: 45 MIN, $16

HOIAN OLD TOWN

民安  國泰

BEACH IN PHU QUOC

## DAY 25-27  PHU QUOC

Time to **catch a flight** from Danang airport and start drinking cocktails in one of the **best beach destinations**. Phu Quoc is an **island** in the **south** of Vietnam, very close to the Cambodian border.

Transportation from
DANANG TO PHU QUOC

 PLANE: $30-80
*Recommended option*

HO CHI
MINH CITY

# 1 month itinerary
## *(11 destinations)*

**DAY 28**  HO CHI MINH CITY

Move on to the **last stop of the trip**. Take advantage of this day to go to the **Cu Chi tunnels** and get to know the city of Saigon

Transportation from
PHU QUOC-HO CHI MINH

 PLANE: $30
*Recommended*

**DAY 29**  MEKONG DELTA

Takng a **tour** is the easiest and fastest way to go to the Mekong Delta. Take a day to check out the impressive **floating market** where locals sell products from their boats. The visit is also noted for its beautiful landscapes and tropical fruit farms.

Transportation from
HO CHI MINH TO MEKONG

*I recommend that you book a tour to go to the Mekong Delta. The trip will be shorter and way more comfrotable.*

 TOUR: 4 HOURS, $15-50

 PLANE: $30-80
*Recommended*

**DAY 30**  HO CHI MINH CITY

Finally, enjoy your last hours in the city having a **drink** at one of the **terraces** in the **city center** and **shopping** before returning home.

MEKONG
DELTA

Best places
to visit

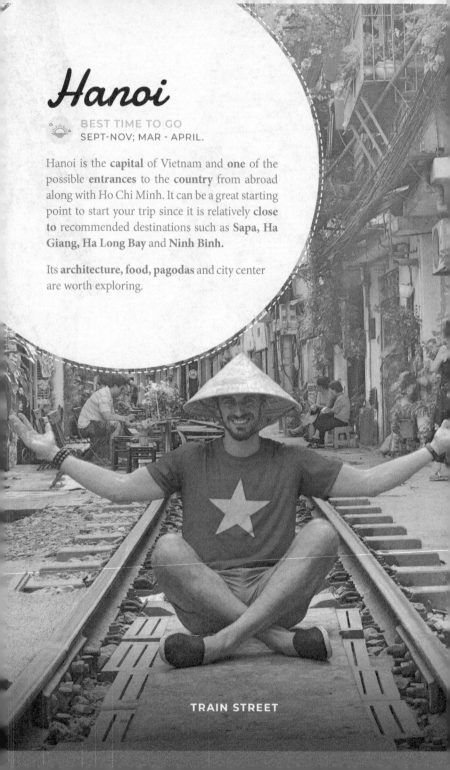

# Hanoi

Hanoi is the **capital** of Vietnam and **one** of the possible **entrances** to the **country** from abroad along with Ho Chi Minh. It can be a great starting point to start your trip since it is relatively **close to** recommended destinations such as **Sapa, Ha Giang, Ha Long Bay** and **Ninh Binh.**

Its **architecture, food, pagodas** and city center are worth exploring.

**TRAIN STREET**

# What to do *Hanoi*

**1.** TRAIN STREET

Spectacular to feel how the **train passes** just **a few centimeters from you**. On that street there are many **cafes** where you can **have a drink** and **see the train passing by**. It is very curious to observe how the establishments move the tables and chairs just a couple of minutes before the train passes.

**2.** HOAN KIEM LAKE

One of the most **famous places in Hanoi**. It is located in the heart of Hanoi, next to the main pedestrian area of the city. You can see the "Turtle Tower", the striking **Huc bridge** and a **temple** on a small island.

**3.** OLD QUARTER

**Lose yourself in the sea of alleys** in this neighborhood that has well-preserved **ancient architecture**. In addition, in this area you can find many **shops, bars, restaurants, cafes** and **hotels**.

At night, there is the '**Ta Hien Beer Street**': the best place to try **street food** and drink beer in Hanoi.

HOAN KIEM LAKE

**4.** LITERATURE TEMPLE

The **most important temple** in the city and the one that best represents Vietnamese architecture. It was the site of the first university in Vietnam.

**5.** HO CHI MINH MAUSOLEUM

It contains the **body** of the independence leader and **founder** of the **Communist Party** of Vietnam, **Ho Chi Minh**. The venue has a strict dress code (shoulders and knees must be covered) and cameras are not allowed.

**6.** WATER PUPPET SHOW

The **show** depicts the **daily life** of **Vietnamese peasants**, **festivals** and country sights.

HO CHI MINH MAUSOLEUM

# What to do *Hanoi*

 *Restaurants*

1. **BÁNH MÌ 25**
   (VIETNAMESE)

2. **HOANG CUISINE**
   (VIETNAMESE)

3. **CAFE GIANG**
   (VIETNAMESE)

4. **IVEGAN SUPERSHOP**

- - - - - - - - - - - - - - - -

 *Hotels*

### HANOI LA SIESTA CENTRAL HOTEL

**$$$$**
Elegant hotel with great views located in the center of the city.

### LITTLE CHARM HANOI HOSTEL

**$**
Central hostel ideal for meeting other travellers.

 **Prices**

$ = UP TO $10
$$ = $11-30
$$$ = $31-60
$$$$ = OVER $61

 *Vegan*

# Sapa

It is located **380 km northwest** of **Hanoi** and close to the **Chinese border**. Sapa is **famous** for its **hills, valleys** and **beautiful landscapes** with **rice fields.** In addition, it is home to the **most famous ethnic tribes** in Vietnam and one of the best areas in the country for **hiking**. You will have a unique experience if you stay in a 'homestay' on the outskirts of the city. Don't forget to **bring warm clothes** if you visit this area.

# What to do *Sapa*

**1.** GO HIKING

Hire a **tour** or **local guide** at your hotel to enjoy the wonderful **landscapes** surrounded by **rice fields between mountains**. In this way, you can also reach villages of ethnic groups in the region.

**2.** STAY IN A 'HOMESTAY'

Live, **eat and sleep** under the same roof as an **ethnic minority**. Homestays are similar to hostels, but unlike hostels, they will immerse you in Vietnamese culture in a more authentic way.

**3.** RENT A MOTORCYCLE AND GET LOST IN THE MOUNTAINS

The landscapes in Sapa are spectacular and you will surely want to **stop every few minutes** to **take photos**.

Stop for a **coffee** at the '**Muong Hoa River Homestay**'. There you have a **spectacular view**: a **river** running through the **valley between terraced rice fields**.

**4.** NIGHT MARKET

Women **dressed** in **traditional costumes** go out every night to the central square of Sapa to **sell handicrafts**.

**5.** CAT CAT TOWN

If you have little time in Sapa, this can be a good option due to its **proximity** to the **city center**. Although the town is a **recreation** of a **typical town** in the area, it is beautiful and well preserved.

**6.** VISIT THE 'LOVE MARKET'

**Every Saturday** men and women from the H'Mong and Red Dao **minorities meet** for the purpose of **finding a partner** in Sapa.

# What to do *Sapa*

 *Restaurants*

1. SKYVIEW RESTAURANT & BAR SAPA(RESTAURANT)

2. OMAR'S NAMASTE (RESTAURANT)

3. RESTAURANT YUMMY (VIETNAMESE)

4. CLASSIC VEGAN SAPA

---

🛏 *Hotels*

### TOPAS ECOLODGE

**$$$$**
Its views of the Hoang Lien Valley will take your breath

### LA BEAUTÉ SAPA

**$$**
We stayed at this homestay and we loved its location, the treatment we received from the family and the fact that we got to know the residents of the community.

FANSIPAN (HIGHEST POINT IN VIETNAM)

# Ha Giang loop

BEST TIME TO GO
MARCH-MAY; SEPTEMBER-OCTOBER

A **little-known destination** for mass tourism. It is gradually gaining popularity. This trip is not a specific point, but a **motorcycle trip** through the **scenic landscapes**. It has departure from the city of Ha Giang.

Get ready to see mountain canyons surrounded by rice terraces and cornfields, **driving through mountain passes** and into destinations where you are stuck in time. You can see women working hard in the fields with their babies on their backs or 9-year-olds riding motorcycles.

# What to do *Ha Giang Loop*

The trip can be done in **2-5 days**, although I recommend at least 4 days to be able to calmly enjoy the trip and stop to take pictures.

### ITINERARY 1
**Start and end** in **Ha Giang** town (loop):
1. Ha Giang - 2. Yen Minh
3. Dong Van - 4. Ma Pi Length Pass
5. Ha Giang

### ITINERARY 2
**Ha Giang - Ban Gioc waterfall**:
1. Ha Giang - 2. Yen Minh
3. Dong Van - 4. Bao Lac.

**1.** MOUNTAIN PASS 'HEAVEN'S GATE'

**2.** MA PI LENG PASS

**3.** TORRE LUNG CU
It is the northernmost point of the country.

**4.** BAN GIOC WATERFALLS
-------------------------------

Remember that the best thing about this destination is not a specific point, but the motorcycle ride, which is truly spectacular. You'll want to stop every 5 minutes to take photos of the scenery.

### How to get a motorcycle?
My friends and I traveled with "**QT Bikes**" (non-sponsored content) in Ha Giang City and had a great experience. If you don't have driving experience, you also have the option of hiring an '**easy rider**', a **motorcycle driver** or **guide** who will take you during the tour of the Ha Giang Loop.

BAN GIOC
WATERFALL

# What to do

*Ha Giang Loop*

 *Hotels*

**YEN BIEN LUXURY HOTEL**
$$$
At  Ha Giang.

**DU GIA CN HOMESTAY**
$
At Yen Minh.

**HOANG NGOC HOTEL**
$
At Dong Van.

**LITTLE YEN'S HOMESTAY**
$
At Meo Vac.

# Halong Bay

 BEST TIME TO GO
FEBRUARY-MAY;
SEPTEMBER-DECEMBER

A **wonder** of **nature** for its **hills scattered** by the **sea**. It is located near the border with China. Just **2 hours from Hanoi**. A must see destination since you will not find another place with such singular beauty in another corner of the world.

# What to do *Halong Bay*

**1.** DO ADVENTURE SPORTS
Ideal for **hiking** to the top of its hills, climbing or **kayaking**.

**2.** EXPLORE CAT BA, THE LARGEST ISLAND IN HALONG
**Explore it** by **bicycle** or **motorcycle**, visit its natural park or simply relax sunbathing on one of its beaches.

**3.** HOUSEBOAT TOUR
Imagine meeting the **people** who work and **live** with their neighbors among **houses that float** in the bay.

**4.** HANG SUNG SOT GROTTOES
The bay is also home to numerous **caves that can be visited**.

**5.** BAY CRUISE
Book a **tour** of **1 or 2 days sailing** between its islets.

**6.** CABLE CAR
See the bay from above with a cable car ride from **Halong city**.

# What to do
*Halong Bay*

 *Restaurants*

1. **MAY CORNER (VIETNAMESE)** $

2. **AVOCADO RESTAURANT** $-$$

3. **LINH DAN RESTAURANT (RESTAURANT)** $-$$

4. **WANDER STATION (BREAKFAST)** $

 *Hotels*

### ROSY CRUISES
**$$$$**
Enjoy the elegance of this cruise around the islets of Halong Bay.

### BBQ HOSTEL HALONG
**$$**
Very good hostel located close to the main attractions.

# Ninh Binh

Not as well known as other parts of Vietnam, but finally getting the recognition it deserves. You will be amazed by its **landscapes** that seem to have been taken from a National Geographic documentary. Ninh Binh is my favorite destination in Vietnam, just **two and a half hours from Hanoi**. Visit between May and July to see the rice fields and lotus flowers.

MUA CAVES

# What to do *Ninh Binh*

**1.** TRAVEL BY BOAT THROUGH TAM COC OR TRANG AN

Beautiful **boat trip through rivers, pagodas, rice fields** and **caves**. Although the two boat rides are beautiful, my favorite is the one in Trang An.

**2.** VIEWS FROM THE TOP OF 'HANG MUA' MOUNTAIN

**Climb** the **more than 500 steps** to enjoy one of the **best viewpoints** in the entire country. It has a spectacular **statue** of a **dragon** at the **top**.

PAGODA-TAM COC RIVER

**3.** BAI DINH PAGODA

**Largest Buddhist temple** in **Southeast Asia**. It stands out for the **thousands** of **Buddha statues** and its beautiful views from the top.

**4.** RENT A MOTORCYCLE OR BICYCLE

Explore its wonderful **landscapes between hills** and **rice fields** where you will have the chance to see buffalo and wild goats.

**5.** BICH DONG PAGODA

Visit one of the **icons** of **Ninh Binh**.

**6.** STAY IN A SUBURBAN HOMESTAY

The city of Ninh Binh does not have any places of interest. **What is truly special** about **Ninh Binh is** its **landscapes** and **nature** on the outskirts of the city. So I recommend you to stay between hills and rice fields.

MUA CAVES

BAI DINH PAGODA

# What to do *Ninh Binh*

TAM COC RIVER

## Restaurants

1. **FATHER COCKING RESTAURANT $**

2. **TRUNG TUYET RESTAURANT $**

3. **BAMBOO BAR AND RESTAURANT (VIETNAMESE) $**

4. **THAO BÉO RESTAURANT BAR (VIETNAMESE) $**

## Hotels

### TRANG AN RIVER VIEW HOMESTAY

$

Surrounded by the beautiful hills of Ninh Binh, rice fields and lotus flowers.

### GREEN MOUNTAIN HOMESTAY

$$

Enjoy its tranquility and terrace with beautiful views.

# Phong Nha

Phong Nha is a **destination for adventurers** seeking nature experiences. The place is famous for having the **largest caves** in the **world** and its **expeditions** through the **jungle**. You can also camp inside these natural wonders. It is no coincidence that Phong Nha was chosen to shoot the movie "King Kong": its landscapes are spectacular and you still won't find as many tourists as in other parts of Vietnam.

# What to do *Phong Nha*

**1.** EXPLORE THE LARGEST CAVES IN THE WORLD

Visit the **largest cave** in the **world** (Son Doong). It costs more than US$3,000. Fortunately, there are other expeditions. You can do **tours from 1 to 4 days** in length for a more reasonable price (**$50-500**). You have to be physically fit and have a sense of adventure to travel through the Vietnamese jungle.

**2.** BOAT TRIP

A **quieter activity**. Take a boat ride and enjoy the wonderful landscapes.

**3.** MOTORCYCLE OR BICYCLE RIDE

The best way to tour Phong Nha. Get to know the area and natural park at your own pace and take photos on its **roads surrounded by jungle**.

**4.** PHONG NHA FARMSTAY

If you prefer a quiet day, I recommend spending the day in this **hotel**. You can go for a **drink** and enjoy its **beautiful pool surrounded** by **rice fields**. They also organize walks in the morning and in the afternoon. Its owner gives talks on the history of Phong Nha and local life.

**5.** DUCK STOP

A surreal activity where you can have a fun time surrounded by geese and an ox named Donald Trump. Believe it or not, it is the **favorite activity** of **many travelers** in Phong Nha!

**6.** VISITA LAS CUEVAS 'PARADISE CAVE' Y 'DARK CAVE'

The 'Paradise Cave' is an **accessible cave** for people of **all ages** and **physical conditions**. You **don't need to go** into the **jungle** to visit it. In addition, in the 'Dark Cave' you can enjoy aquatic activities.

*Tip*
The best agencies to book a tour in Phong Nha are 'Oxalis' and 'Jungle Boss'.

# What to do *Phong Nha*

 *Restaurants*

1. MOMMA D'S ROOFTOP $$

2. LOUNGE & SOIREE (RESTAURANT) $

3. PHONG NHA COFFEE STATION (BREAKFAST) $

4. NGUYEN SHACK ART CAFÉ (BREAKFAST) $

 *Hotels*

### CARAMBOLA BUNGALOW

$$
Excellent hotel located on the outskirts of Phong Nha. It is a hotel

### FARMSTAY

$$$$
Very cozy cabins located next to the Phong Nha river.

 *Prices*

$ = UP TO $10
$$ = $11-30
$$$ = $31-60
$$$$ = OVER $61

NATIONAL PARK (ENTRY POINT)

49

# Hue

🌅 BEST TIME TO GO
JANUARY-AUGUST

Hue is one of the most historic cities in Vietnam, just **2 and a half hours from Danang.** It conserves **temples, pagodas** and **mausoleums** of the Nguyen dynasty that ruled Vietnam during the **19th century** and in which Hue was its capital.

IMPERIAL CITY

# What to do *Hue*

**TU DUC TUMBS**

**1.** ABANDONED AMUSEMENT PARK (HO THUY TIEN)

8 km from the Imperial City, there is an abandoned amusement park and the **most famous dragon** in Vietnam's traveling **photographs**. You have to pay about $2 to the security guard to let you in.

**2.** IMPERIAL CITY

It often **reminds** visitors of the **Forbidden City** in **Beijing** for its **walls and temples**. It was the **residence** of the **emperor** during the Nguyen dynasty, when Hue was the capital of Vietnam.

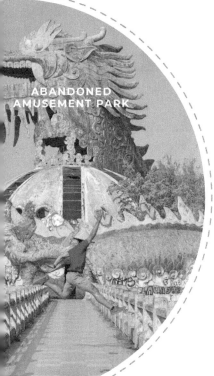

**ABANDONED AMUSEMENT PARK**

**3.** THIEN MU PAGODA

Possibly the **most visited pagoda** in **Hue**.

**4.** VISIT THE TOMBS OF THE EMPERORS

The **tombs** of '**Khai Dinh**' are the **most visited.** There you have some **spectacular statues of** emperors and the army made of **stone**. The tombs of '**Tu Duc**' are also **worth visiting**.

**5.** BACH MA NATIONAL PARK

At 1450 meters above level. You can take a **walk through** the **jungle** and enjoy **waterfalls, lakes** and beautiful views.

**6.** SKY BAR VINPEARL HOTEL

It is the **only skyscraper** in the **city**. There you can go have a **drink** with **great views** of Hue.

# What to do *Hue*

 *Restaurants*

**1.** COZY RESTAURANT & CAFE $

**2.** SERENE CUISINE RES-TAURANT $-$$

 *Hotels*

### ALBA SPA HOTEL

$$$
Elegant hotel located in the center of Hue.

### EVA HOMESTAY

$$
Very attentive employees who will help you plan your stay in Hue.

# Danang

As in the case of Hanoi, Danang can be another of your stops since it is a **short distance** from **Hoian, Hue** and has one of the **most important airports** in the country. In addition, it has excursions that are really worthwhile (such as the **Golden bridge**) and some of the **best beaches** in the country.

DRAGON BRIDGE

# What to do *Danang*

MARBLE MOUNTAINS

### 4. GOLDEN BRIDGE

One of the most spectacular bridges ever built. It has **giant hands** that **appear** to **hold up** the **bridge**. It is part of an **amusement park** that you can only **access by cable car**.

### 5. DRAGON BRIDGE

Spectacular **dragon-shaped bridge** that stretches 666 meters. If you are passing through on the weekend, go to its night show at **9 pm on Saturday** or **Sunday** where you can see the **dragon spit fire** and **water**

### 1. BEACHES

**Some** of the **best beaches** in Vietnam are in Danang. In addition, you can **surf** almost all year round.

### 6. LINH UNG PAGODA

Nice **pagoda** with great **ocean views**. The temple has a large Buddhist statue and several temples concentrated on top of a mountain.

### 2. MOUNTAINS OF THE 5 ELEMENTS (MARBLE MOUNTAINS)

Just 9 km from Danang, enjoy these **mountains** that have **caves** and **temples inside**.

### 3. HAI VAN MOUNTAIN PASS (HAI VAN PASS)

**Rent a motorcycle** and enjoy the spectacular landscapes with **views** of the **sea**. It was one of my favorite excursions in my trip through Vietnam.

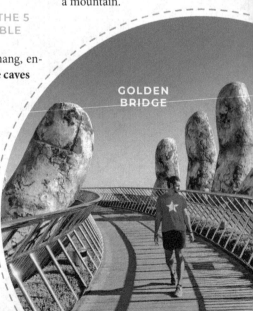

GOLDEN BRIDGE

# What to do *Danang*

 *Restaurants*

 *Hotels*

1. **ROOTS PLANTS BASED CAFE (BREAKFAST) $**

2. **ROM KITCHEN (VIETNAMESE) $**

3. **CITRON RESTAURANT (RESTAURANT) $$$**

**NANG CAPSULE HOSTEL**
$
If you have always dreamed of sleeping in a capsule hotel, here is a very good, cheap and comfortable option. Enjoy lighting and sound cancellation.

**HAIAN BEACH HOTEL & SPA**
$$$
Enjoy the incredible views of the infinity pool.

LINH UNG PAGODA

# Hoian

**BEST TIME TO GO**
**FEBRUARY-AUGUST**

Hoian is the **favorite city** for **many travelers** when visiting Vietnam. It is a perfect destination that perfectly **combines history, architecture, gastronomy** and **beaches**. It is only 45 **minutes from Danang**. Here you can take the photos with the most flavor of Vietnam of the entire trip.

**NIGHT MARKET**

# What to do *Hoian*

### 1. VISIT THE JAPANESE BRIDGE

The **most representative bridge** in Hoian whose construction dates back to the **16th century**.

### 2. GET A TAILORED SUIT

Hoian was for several centuries a destination for cloth trade. Today it is possible to get a **tailored suit** with very **little money** in just **24 hours**.

### 3. VISIT THE NIGHT MARKET

The city is transformed at night with **hundreds** of **colored lanterns** that illuminate the **streets** and canals of the city. In the **market**, too, you can also buy **handicrafts**, clothes and try **street food**.

### 4. NIGHT BOAT RIDE

It is a very beautiful experience since at night the **city** is **illuminated** with **colored lanterns**.

### 5. BEACHES

Hoian has **beaches very close to** the **old town** where you can relax and sunbathe. My favorite in Hoian is An Bang.

### 6. HISTORICAL CENTER

Hoian old town is a gem. It's worth wandering around aimlessly. Its **old houses**, **architecture**, **colors** and lanterns decorating the houses will fascinate you.

Don't miss the opportunity to visit the **'Fujian Assembly Hall'**. It is the most beautiful temple in Hoian, located in the old town.

JAPANESE BRIDGE

57

# What to do *Hoian*

 *Restaurants*

*1.* **ROSIE'S CAFE
(BREAKFAST)$**

*2.* **AVOS & MANGO
(BREAKFAST)$**

*3.* **BANH MI PHUONG
(VIETNAMESE)$**

*4.* **LE CABANON HOIAN
(RESTAURANT)$**

*5.* **LITTLE FAIFO
(RESTAURANT)$-$$**

 *Hotels*

**SOUTHERN HOTEL HOIAN**

$$
Accommodation near the old
town.

**AIRA BOUTIQUE
HOI AN HOTEL & SPA**

$$$
If you prefer to be near the
beach during your stay in
Hoian, this is your option.

# Ho Chi Minh City

With 9 million inhabitants, Ho Chi Minh City is the largest in Vietnam. **Modern** destination and the **financial center** of the country. **Formerly called Saigon**, the city will serve as your **base** in the south if you **travel** to the **Mekong Delta** and the **Cu Chi tunnels** or **Phu Quoc**.

Popular tourist destination that combines French colonial architecture with pagodas and **modern skyscrapers**.

LANDMARK 81 BUILDING

# What to do
## Ho Chi Minh City

**1.** WAR MUSEUM
Probably the **best museum** in **Vietnam**. It portrays the **horrors** of **war** and displays military machinery such as tanks and planes.

**2.** BEN THANH MARKET
The perfect place to **buy** your **gifts** and souvenirs from your trip to Vietnam. Don't forget to **negotiate prices**!

**3.** NGUYEN HUE PEDESTRIAN STREET
This street is the soul of the city. At **night**, when temperatures drop, it is worth strolling down this street, having a **beer** and trying **street food**.

Next to this street you can visit the 'Cafe apartments': an old building where its homes are now occupied by cafes and fashion stores.

MEKONG DELTA

**4.** POST OFFICE, NOTRE DAME CATHEDRAL AND REUNIFICATION PALACE
Located in the **historic center** and visited as symbols of war or **architecture** of **French colonialism**.

**5.** HAVE A DRINK IN A SKYSCRAPER
District 1 of Ho Chi Minh has many bars, **terraces** and **spectacular views** of the city. Drop by for a **drink** in the evening.

**6.** BU VIEN STREET
This really is not an experience for everyone. But if you are curious to see hell on earth, stop by the 'Bu Vien' **bar area**. You can see children doing fire shows, people drinking, bars with deafening music and many **surreal scenes**. They will fascinate you.

REUNIFICATION PALACE

# What to do
## *Ho Chi Ming City*

 *Restaurants*

**1.** CAFE MARCEL
(BREAKFAST)$-$$

**2.** SHAMBALLA
VEGETARIAN
RESTAURANT &
TEA HOUSE $$-$$$

**3.** BUN BO NAM
BO - BA BA
(VIETNAMESE)$

**4.** MAM 148
(VIETNAMESE)$

**5.** 4 P'S
$-$$

 *Hotels*

### LA VELA SAIGON HOTEL

$$

This hotel is really worth it for
the 360° views from the pool
on its terrace.

### BLAND LANDMARK PLUS
### LUXURY RESIDENCE

$$$

If you prefer a little more luxury
at a good price in an apartment.

# Phu Quoc

Located on an **island** in the **south** of Vietnam and with **idyllic temperatures** all **year round**. Phu Quoc is home to some of the best beaches in Vietnam and a destination for tourists looking to escape city life. The easiest way to get there is via a flight from Saigon.

# What to do *Phu Quoc*

### BEACHES

**1.** Phu Quoc has possibly the **best beaches** in the entire **country**. Long Beach, Bai So, Ong Lang, Bai Thom and Bai Dai are some of the best. The island also has **good spots** for **diving** and **snorkeling**.

### PHU QUOC PRISON MUSEUM

**2.** It was built by **French colonialism**. It was one of the jails where Viet Cong and North Vietnamese prisoners were imprisoned and tortured.

### HON THOM CABLE CAR

**3.** My favorite attraction in Phu Quoc. Its **8 km route** is impressive, its height (not suitable for people with vertigo), immense cement columns and **spectacular views** of all the islands of the **archipelago.**

### RENT A MOTORCYCLE

**4.** It is advisable to **rent** a **motorcycle** to **move easily**. The island is too big to explore on foot or by taxi.

### STARFISH BEACH

**5.** A paradise where you can be **surrounded** by **starfish**. Although away from most tourist locations, you can **reach** this **beach** by **motorcycle**.

### HO QUOC TEMPLE

**6.** Without a doubt, the most **beautiful temple** on the island. It has **spectacular views** of the **ocean**. The best time to visit is at dawn.

# What to do
## *Phu Quoc*

 *Restaurants*

**1.** THE SPICE HOUSE
AT CASSIA COTTAGE
(VIETNAMESE)$$

**2.** OCEAN BEACH
BAR & CLUB
(RESTAURANT)$-$$

**3.** THE EMBASSY
(BREAKFAST)$

**4.** HOLLYPOLLY
SMOOTHIE BOWLBAR
(BREAKFAST)$

HO QUOC
PAGODA

 *Hotels*

| DUSIT PRINCESS MOONRISE BEACH RESORT | 9 STATION HOSTEL PHU QUOC |
|---|---|
| $$ | $$$ |
| Fantastic beachfront hotel with infinity pool. | Comfortable, modern and quiet hotel. It is an excellent value for its price. |

Unique

Experiences

# Explore the largest cave in the world
## *Song Doong*

This cave was **discovered** just a few years ago (**2009**) in Phong Nha. One of its grottoes is so large that it can hold an entire block of 40 Manhattan buildings.

Since they began exploring their territory in 1990, **170 caves** have been **discovered** in the Phong Nha Nature Park. The most impressive thing is that **70%** of the natural area is still **to be explored**.

TheSon Doong experience lasts **4 days** and costs **$3,000.** In the adventure you have the possibility of **camping inside** the **caves**, **swimming** in its **underground rivers** and going **deep** into the Vietnamese **jungle**.

If you can't afford the cost of the Son Doong experience, there are **other similar tours**. They last **1-4 days** and **prices start** at $50.

 $3,000

 PHONG NHA

# Halong Bay Castaways
## *Ha Long Bay*

This is one experience that you **will enjoy** especially **if you** are between **18 to 30 years**. Imagine going to a **small island** in Ha Long Bay for **24-48 hours** where there is only a **beach**, cabins to sleep in, **young people, parties, alcohol** and **few rules**. During the morning and afternoon, there is also the possibility of kayaking and playing volleyball.

This **experience** is **called 'Castaways'** and is organized by Vietnam Backpacker Hostels.

 $139-199

 HALONG BAY

HOMESTAY IN SAPA

# 3. 'Homestay' with a local family in *Sapa*

One of the most popular experiences in Vietnam is to **spend** your **vacation** with a **family** from one of the **Vietnamese minority ethnic groups**.

I recommend that you get out of your comfort zone, don't go to a hotel and stay with a local family. Their huts are usually **decorated** in a **traditional way** and you will be able to taste delicious **Vietnamese food** while learning more about their culture.

In addition, they offer the possibility of **excursions** to the less traveled and most **beautiful places** in Sapa.

 $5-75

 SAPA

# Motorcycle trips

Vietnam is still a relatively new country to mass tourism and it has many new places to explore.

There are regions where foreign tourists have barely visited and where the locals are surprised to see you.

In addition to the **Ha Giang loop** (**north** of the country) and '**Hai Van pass**' (in **Danang**), there are other trips to make by motorcycle in Vietnam. Don't forget that it is the main transport in this country and the best way to get around when at a new destination.

 $6-9

 HA GIANG

# Hike to the top of Vietnam:
## *Fansipan*

**BUDHIST TEMPLE IN FANSIPAN**

The **highest point** of the Indochina peninsula and Vietnam, at 3,**147 meters** above sea level.

**Hiking** to the top takes **one or two days,** although remember that you can go up by **cable car** in just **30 minutes**.

It is **mandatory** to **hire** a **guide** for the ascent. My experience with this agency (www.theterrible-tourguide.com) was unbeatable (recommendation not sponsored).

💰 $100

📍 SAPA

# 6. Topas Ecolodge in *Sapa*

One of the favorite places for travelers in Vietnam.

The **boutique hotel** has **fantastic views** of the **mountains** and rice fields, especially from its **panoramic pool**.

If you cannot afford to stay in this hotel, you still have the option to purchase a **ticket** to **spend** the **day** on its terrace and **pool**.

VIEWS FROM TOPAS ECOLODGE

 $150/NIGHT
$18 DAY PASS

 SAPA

# 7. Cu Chi War tunnels
## *Ho Chi Minh*

Just **an hour from Saigon**, you can visit this **250 km** interconnected **tunnel** system. They were **used** by Viet Cong guerrillas in the **war** as **hideouts**, hospitals, and storage for weapons and food. You can even try to explore a small part of these tunnels and wonder how they managed to survive such narrow and hot hiding places.

The **best way** to visit this place is by taking a **tour from Saigon**, since it is a bit complicated and inconvenient to get there by public transport..

 $6 - $12

 HO CHI MINH CITY

# Cooking lesson

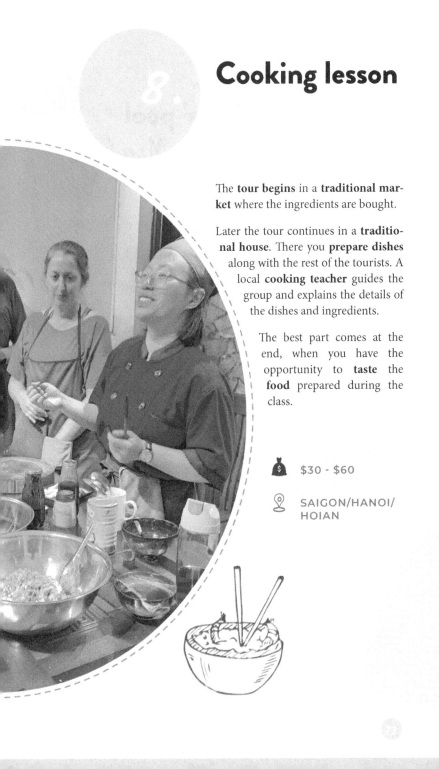

The **tour begins** in a **traditional market** where the ingredients are bought.

Later the tour continues in a **traditional house**. There you **prepare dishes** along with the rest of the tourists. A local **cooking teacher** guides the group and explains the details of the dishes and ingredients.

The best part comes at the end, when you have the opportunity to **taste** the **food** prepared during the class.

$30 - $60

SAIGON/HANOI/HOIAN

# 9. 'La Vela' pool
## *Ho Chi Minh*

One of the **pools** with **best views** in **Vietnam**. It is located in the city of **Saigon**.

You can buy a day pass to enjoy its infinity pool withalmost **360º views**. There they also have a bar and restaurant where you can **eat** or have a few **drinks**.

 $10

 HO CHI MINH CITY

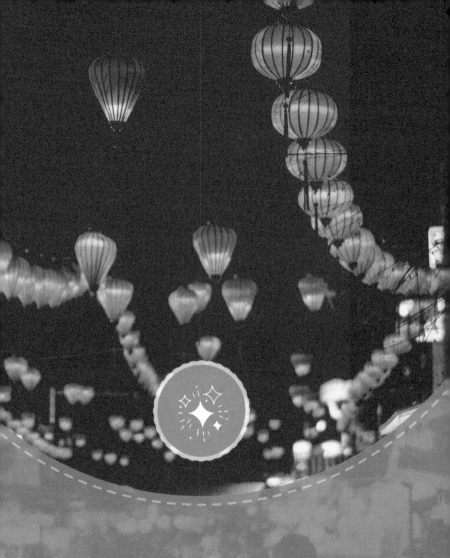

# Best in
# Vietnam

# Best beaches

Vietnam is not a country with spectacular beaches. At least, it is difficult to find beaches with emerald water and white sand like the beautiful beaches of Thailand or the Philippines. Anyway, here are some of the **best destinations** or **beaches** in Vietnam.

# Best in Vietnam: *Beaches*

**1.** STARFISH BEACH
Starfish beach is, as its name indicates, a beach with a **multitude** of **starfish**. Not yet very popular since it was **discovered** in **2014**.

The **best way** to visit it is by **renting** a **motorcycle**, since there is no public transport and part of the road is sand and stone. Don't forget when taking your photos: not to touch or take them out of water. They are animals that need water to live and suffer from being out of it and being touched.

Finally, remember that you will **only** be able to see starfish **between** the months of **November and April**.

LONG BEACH

**2.** LONG BEACH
Probably the **most popular beach** on **Phu Quoc** Island.

There you can find **many hotels, restaurants** and **bars**. If what you are looking for is a lot of ambience and being in contact with more people, this is the right place.

**WHERE** Phu Quoc ☀ **BEST** Nov - Apr

**WHERE** Phu Quoc ☀ **BEST** Nov - Apr

**3.** CUA DAI
This beach is located just **5 km from Hoian**.

It is a very **popular beach** among **tourists**. There are plenty of places to eat and places offering **drinks** and handicrafts. You can also **surf**.

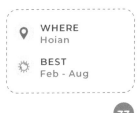
**WHERE** Hoian
☀ **BEST** Feb - Aug

# Best in Vietnam: *Beaches*

### 4. AN BANG

An Bang beach is one of the few in the area that is not too affected by human action. It is a **less touristy** beach than Cua Dai.

There you can find various **seafood restaurants** and **alternative bars**. It also has good views of Danang Bay and the Cham Islands. In addition, it is a good place to learn to **surf**.

| WHERE | BEST |
|-------|------|
| Hoian | Feb - Ago |

BEACH IN HOIAN

### 5. MY KHE

It is the **most popular beach** in all of **Vietnam**.

It is perfect to practice or start **surfing**. It is **located** in the **heart** of **Danang**. It has **many hotels** and **restaurants** along its coast.

| WHERE | BEST |
|--------|------|
| Danang | May - Oct |

### 6. NON NHUOC

**20 minutes from** the center of **Danang**, is this **quiet beach**. Its waters are very clean and its **sand is white**.

Along its 5 km you can find **luxury resorts** and **elegant restaurants**. It is also a good place to **surf**.

'MI KHE' BEACH

| WHERE | BEST |
|--------|------|
| Danang | May - Oct |

# Best scenic viewpoints

Here are the best observation points in Vietnam:

# Best in Vietnam:
## *Viewpoints*

**1.** HANG MUA

The **500 steps** to the **top** are really worth it. From the top of the mountain you can enjoy **2 observation points** with views of rice fields and the Tam Coc River.

The most spectacular of them has **panoramic views next** to a spectacular **dragon statue**.

| WHERE | PRICE |
|-------|-------|
| Ninh Binh | $4 |

**2.** BAI THO

It is a very difficult place to access since you have to go through the home of an elderly woman. In addition to paying her a tip, if she's in a bad mood she may not let you in.

Also, you have to do a bit of **climbing** and a **20-minute walk**. So I don't recommend it for people with fear of heights.

Anyway, if you manage to get to this place, it will be one of your favorite moments in the trip to Vietnam.

This is the address to find the access point: 89 Hàng Nồi, Thành phố Hạ Long, Quảng Ninh, Việt Nam.

| WHERE | PRICE |
|-------|-------|
| Phu quoc | $4 |

# Best in Vietnam:
## *Viewpoints*

TEMPLES IN FANSIPAN

### 3. FANSIPAN

The **highest point** in Vietnam (**3,143 meters**) that you can reach by **hiking or cable car**. If you are in Sapa for a short time or don't feel like doing sports, I recommend the cable car. Your journey takes about 30 minutes.

The views during the trip are impressive. In addition, on **top** of Fansipan there are some spectacular **Buddhist temples** and **statues**.

| WHERE | PRICE |
|-------|-------|
| Sapa | $25 |

### 4. LANDMARK 81

In the city of **Saigon** is the **tallest building** in all of **Southeast Asia** (460 meters high).

I recommend that you go when the sun is going down for the beautiful sunset.

**WHERE**
Ho Chi Minh

**PRICE**
$35

LANDMARK 81

# Best in Vietnam: *Viewpoints*

**5.** LOTTE CENTER
The building has **61 floors**. Located in **Hanoi** (capital of Vietnam). Although not as spectacular as the Landmark 81 tower in Ho Chi Minh City, it has a panoramic view and **glass floor** that will take your breath away.

WHERE
Hanoi

PRICE
$4

**6.** CABLE CAR ON PHU QUOC ISLAND
**8 km cable car** ride along the Phu Quoc archipelago.

People with vertigo can have a hard time since it rises to about **175 meters high**. From the top you have views of the islands of Phu Quoc. From there you can take some of the most spectacular photos of your trip to Vietnam.

WHERE
Phu Quoc

PRICE
$4

**7.** MA PI LENG MOUNTAIN PASS
Probably the place with the most beautiful views in the 'Ha Giang loop' motorcycle adventure.

**During** the **Ma Pi mountain pass**, you have **several cafes**. You can stop to contemplate the landscape while you take a break and Vietnamese coffee.

Anyway, this is a trip where you have panoramic views every few kilometers.

WHERE
Ha Giang Loop

PRICE
$4

CABLE CAR
PHU QUOC

# Transportation

**Traveling** in **Vietnam** is **not difficult** at all since you can get around with a **variety** of **transport: motorcycle or taxi** within the **cities; vans, buses, trains** and **planes** for **long distance**. With 'Google Maps' you can get an idea of the time and distances between different locations.

Except for the Vietnamese New Year (called TET), transportation is always available and you don't need to book your tickets in advance.

# Public *Transportation*

It is very **uncommon** for **tourists** to take **public buses** in the cities. It is **difficult** to understand how it works and **taxis** are **cheap** and faster.

In **Hanoi** the **subway** is already a reality. It **opened** in **2021**. In Saigon, it is still under construction.

## TRAINS

 Traveling by **train** can be a **unique, safe** and **economical** experience. In addition, you can save spending the night in a hotel if you travel on a **sleeper overnight train**.

There is a **line** from the **south** in **Saigon to Sapa**, passing through the capital, Hanoi. There are **4 types** of **seats** on trains:

1. WOODEN SEAT: The **cheapest**, most **uncomfortable** and may be filled with passengers.

2. SOFT SEAT: Similar to airplanes and very **comfortable**.

3. SEMI-SOFT BED: There are **4 bunk beds per room**. Good option for long or **overnight trips**.

4. SOFT BED: It is the **most expensive** option of the four, but it is still economical. The bunk beds are **comfortable**, especially for long distances.

They have food service, bathrooms and some are equipped with air conditioning and Wi-Fi.

To **book transportation** in Vietnam, the **best option** is **BookaWay**.

On this platform you can find all the routes and means of transport in Vietnam. In addition, the page shows you a **comparison** of **prices** and **number of hours** between the different destinations.

*Tip*
Remember to take care of your belongings during the bus and train journey. Thefts are common.

# Public *Transportation*

## NIGHT BUSES (SLEEPER BUS)

It really is a different experience to travel on these sleeper buses. They **look like discos on wheels** since they are illuminated with neon lights.

Although they are very **cheap**, think twice before traveling on these buses: the bunks are made for the size of a Vietnamese and are very **uncomfortable** as they have little space for the **legs**.

Be aware that some **drivers drive crazy** compared to western standards.

### AIRPLANES

Vietnam has 4 **airlines:** Jetstar, Vietjet, Bamboo Airways and **Vietnam Airlines.**

**Jetstar** and **Vietjet** are **low cost** airlines and you can easily find flights with them from 25 to 50 dollars. Although remember, the vast majority of your flights are delayed. I repeat, the VAST majority!

**Bamboo Airways** and **Vietnam Airways** are not the cheapest airlines. However, they are **more organized** airlines and without so many delays.

### PRIVATE CAR (TAXI)

For **short distances**, it may be the **fastest** and **most comfortable** way to travel. However, unless the vehicle is full, it can be **a bit expensive**.

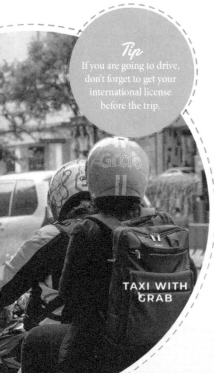

*Tip*
If you are going to drive, don't forget to get your international license before the trip.

TAXI WITH GRAB

# Public *Transportation*

### RENT A MOTORCYCLE

**Recommended option** to get around in **all destinations except Saigon** and **Hanoi** (there is **a lot of traffic** and it can be overwhelming).

It is an **economical option**, but not recommended if you don't have previous experience driving this type of vehicle. It will allow you to **see Vietnam from another perspective**.

### GRAB (TAXI APP)

It is quite an experience to travel by motorcycle with the Grab taxi app. Although you can also request a **car**, I recommend the experience of getting on a **motorcycle** taxi to see the city from another point of view. Also it's very cheap.

It is only **available in big cities** like Hanoi, Danang, Hoian and Ho Chi Minh.

### VAN (LUXURY VAN LIMOUSINE)

It is my **preferred way** to travel **short distances** in Vietnam. The **seats** are wide and **comfortable**. It's **fast** and usually **quite cheap**.

Must know
in Vietnam

# Currency and costs

Vietnam is **one** of the **cheapest countries** in the **world** to travel to. If you get a cheap plane ticket, the rest of the costs such as booking accommodation, buying food and tickets to tourist attractions will be very cheap compared to most countries.

 **CURRENCY**
The currency in Vietnam is called 'Vietnamese Dong' (**VND**). Its equivalence to the **Euro** and **Dollar** is about **25,000 dong**. As the dong always moves in very high quantities, you will have the opportunity to feel like a millionaire during your stay in Vietnam.

There are **bills from 1,000 to 500,000 VND**. The use of coins is rare.

There are 6 ways to get local currency:

1. BEFORE ARRIVING IN VIETNAM

2. AUTOMATED TELLER MACHINES (ATMS)

3. AIRPORT

4. MONEY EXCHANGE SHOPS

5. JEWELERS AND GOLD SHOPS

6. HOTELS

It is advisable to change money before arrival. This way you can get used to the currency and have the opportunity to make small purchases when you arrive in Vietnam.

|  | ADVANTAGES | DISADVANTAGES |
| --- | --- | --- |
| In your country | Have some money ready when you arrive in Vietnam | They don't have good exchange rates |
| Automated Teller Machines (ATMs) | Available in all the cities. I recommend this | Fees and commissions |
| Airport | Having some money ready when you arrive in Vietnam | Unfavorable exchange rate |
| Currency exchange shops | They offer one of the best exchange rates | Only available in big cities |
| Jewelers and shops for buying and selling gold | One of the best exchange rates and trustworthy places | They can only be found in Ho Chi Minh and Hanoi |
| Hotels | One of the most comfortable options | Only the largest hotels offer this service |

# Currency - Costs

Once in the country, the **easiest option** is to **withdraw money** at **ATMs** that can be identified with the acronym ATM (Automatic Transfer Machine). Although in all the cities that I recommend there are ATMs, take some cash since you can't pay with a card in all hotels or establishments.

Although it may seem surprising, you can also get cash in jewelers and gold shops in Hanoi (in the historic center, "Old quarter", Hang Bo and Ha Trung streets) and Ho Chi Minh (next to Ben Thanh market) .

*Advice*
Before your trip begins, consider costs such as visas, vaccinations, and flights.

## TIPPING

Tipping is **not part of the culture** of the country. However, they often greatly appreciate small tips since their salaries are very low.

The exception is usually guided trips and tours. A small amount of money is usually given to the bus driver or the gentlemen who row the Tam Coc (Ninh Binh) boat ride.

| PRICE IN DOLLARS | LOW BUDGET | MEDIUM BUDGET | HIGH BUDGET |
|---|---|---|---|
| Hotels | 4 | 20 | 65 |
| Food | 10 | 20 | 40 |
| Transportation | 5 | 10 | 20 |
| Entrance Tickets | 3 | 6 | 9 |
| Trips | 5 | 10 | 20 |
| TOTAL | $26.5 | $66 | $154 |

# Currency *and costs*

### PRICE OF A ROOM

Finding **accommodation** in Vietnam is **easy** and **cheap**. Hotels and hostels are available for **all budgets**: beds in **shared hostel rooms from $3**, **private rooms from $10** or even **luxury resorts from $40**.

### TRANSPORTATION COST

Traveling by **bus or train** in Vietnam is usually the **cheapest** option. For **short distances**, if you travel with a higher budget, going by van (**van limousine**) or **taxi** is the **fastest** option.

Finally, keep in mind that Vietnam is a country with more than **3,000 km of coastline**, so it is convenient to go by **plane** for **long trips**. There are low-cost airlines that offer **flights from $30**.

### COST OF FOOD AND DRINKS

Vietnam has a varied and rich gastronomy. In addition, **eating** in this country can be **very cheap**. You can eat a 'banh mi' (Vietnamese sandwich) for 12,000 VND (**$0.4**) or its most famous dish, 'pho', for just **$1.5**.

Drinking in Vietnam is also very cheap. The prices of a **beer** range from **0.5 to $2.5**.

### AUTOMATED TELLER MACHINES (ATMS)

If you travel with a **Mastercard, Visa** or **American Express** card you will have **no problem** getting money in Vietnam. **All cities** have **ATMs,** and **most establishments accept** payment by **card**.

# Currency *and costs*

Traveling in Vietnam can be even
cheaper if you follow these **tips**:

**1.** **Travel like a local**. Travel by **train** or **bus** between cities or '**Grab bike**' within the city.

**2.** Travel in **low season** (June to August or December to January).

**3.** Try to **negotiate prices** in markets. They can be inflated up to 80%.

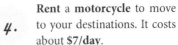

STREET FOOD POINT

NOODLES AND EGGS SOUP

**4.** **Rent** a **motorcycle** to move to your destinations. It costs about **$7/day**.

**5.** If you travel with little money, I recommend that you go to **hostels** with **shared rooms**, you can find a bed **from $3**. There are also single rooms for $10 a night.

**6.** **Try** the **local cuisine**: Vietnamese food is **delicious** and **very cheap**.

**7.** Try **not** to **travel** during the **Vietnamese New Year** called TET (**late January/early February**). **Prices** are **higher** and all destinations are full of people.

# Hotels

Booking a **hotel** for your trip to Vietnam is very **simple** and you can find accommodation for **all budgets**. If you travel **without much money** you can book accommodation in **hostels** or 'homestays', which offer beds in shared rooms or **private rooms** for around **$10**. If you prefer a more luxurious place, you can book rooms in **resorts from $40**. Remember, Vietnam is **one** of the **cheapest countries** to **travel** to in the world.

Booking a hostel, homestay or hotel online is very simple.

On the **Agoda** or **Booking platforms** you can book several nights in a row in advance. In most cases you can even cancel your stay in the event of an unforeseen event.

### HOTEL/RESORT

For **luxury accommodation** in hotels or beach resorts, there is a range of prices from as low as **$40 to $500** per **night**.

### HOSTELS

Vietnam has many hostels where you can find bed or private rooms from **3 to 50 dollars** per night. If you travel alone and want to **meet** other **travelers**, it is undoubtedly the **best option**.

# Hotels

### HOMESTAY

A **unique way** to stay in Vietnam. Local and **ethnic minority families** will open the doors of **their house** for you so you can **spend** the **night**. Especially recommended option in the north of Vietnam, where they can show you beautiful and hidden places to tourists. Its price range goes from **5 to 75 dollars**.

### ASK FOR HOTELS WHEN YOU ARRIVE AT YOUR DESTINATION

A less organized way of traveling is to directly **ask** for accommodation once you **arrive** at your **destination**. Since there are **plenty** of **accommodations**, you probably won't have a problem finding a place to sleep.

### AIRBNB

In the vast majority of destinations in Vietnam you can find accommodation on Airbnb, with prices from **20 to 500 dollars**.

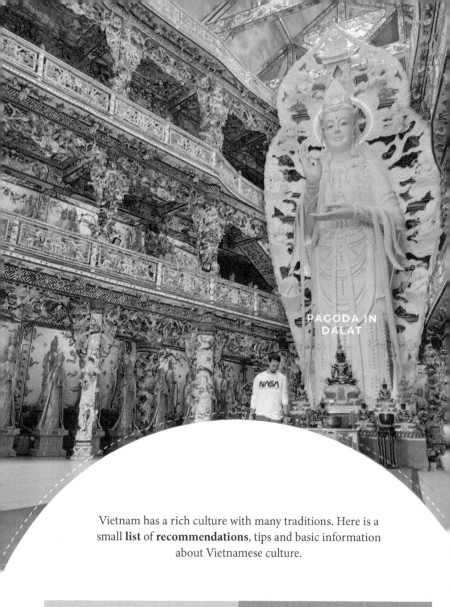

PAGODA IN DALAT

Vietnam has a rich culture with many traditions. Here is a small **list** of **recommendations**, tips and basic information about Vietnamese culture.

| DO'S | DONT'S |
|---|---|
| *Cover knees and shoulders in temples* | *Do not speak about Politics* |
| *Take off the shoes when entering a house* | *Avoid intense displays of affection in public* |
| *Bargain prices in the markets* | *Do not take photos in military places* |

*Culture*

## BASIC INFORMATION

**1.** **Vietnamese official language** of Vietnam. Although in some corners of the country, certain minorities speak **other languages** such as H'Mông, Nùng, Khmer, Cham and Mường.

**2.** Vietnam is a **secular state**, but the **main religion** is Buddhism.

**3.** Vietnam **borders China** to the **north**, **Laos** to the **northwest** and **Cambodia** to the **southwest**. It has an extensive coastline washed by the South China Sea.

**4.** **Hanoi** is the **capital since** the **reunification** of North and South Vietnam in **1976**. **Ho Chi Minh City (formerly called Saigon)** is its **financial capital** and the most modern city in the country.

**5.** **Vietnam** is a Socialist Republic. The lleadership belongs to the **Communist Party**. It elects its new leader without elections every 5 years.

# Safety in Vietnam

**1.** Be especially **careful** about theft of **bags** and **phones** in **Saigon**. It is common in the city center to have your belongings **stolen** by a thief on a **motorcycle**.

**2.** **Use** the 'Grab' **app** to request a taxi, especially **from** the **airport**. A trip from the airport terminal can be about 5-10 dollars with the app. Street taxis can have manipulate the meter.

**3.** It is important to keep in mind that you arrive in a country with an **authoritarian regime** where freedom of speech is very limited. **Locals** usually **avoid talking** about **politics**.

**4.** Don't forget to protect yourself against mosquito bites with insect repellent. Remember that there is dengue and malaria (even in big cities).

**5.** If you travel to **rural areas**, **don't get lost** on less traveled roads as there are still **unexploded bombs** from the **war**.

**6.** **Avoid contact** with **stray dogs**. It is not unreasonable that they can bite you with the risk of transmitting **rabies**.

**7.** Although **street food** is generally safe, keep in mind that **food poisoning** in Southeast Asia is common. Take diarrhea tablets.

**8.** Although there are pedestrian crossings and traffic lights, the Vietnamese often ignore them. Here are a series of **tricks** to easily **cross** the **street** in the traffic chaos in Hanoi and Ho Chi Minh:

• **Cross** at the **same time** as the **locals** and to their right side.

• Take **small steps** while watching the traffic on your left. The motorcycles will dodge you.

• **Extend your left arm** and open the palm of your hand as you cross the street.

Anyway, **crime** in **Vietnam** is **very low**. It is an ideal country for a family trip or even for women traveling alone.

Also remember that in case of any problem, ask the locals for help. There will always be someone who speaks English and gives you a hand.

# Basic words
## *in Vietnamese*

Even though you won't learn Vietnamese in 2 days, it's always nice to arrive in a new country and use a few words in the local language. You can **learn** some **Vietnamese** with this **free app: Duolingo**.

| | |
|---|---|
| *Xin Chào* (sin chow) | HELLO |
| *Cảm Ơn* (gam un) | THANK YOU |
| *Dạ / Không* (yah / comb) | YES / NO |
| *Xin Lỗi* (sin loy) | I AM SORRY |
| *Ngon quá* (ngon wha) | DELICIOUS! |
| *Bao nhiêu?* (bow nyew) | HOW MUCH? |
| *Mắc quá* (mack wha) | TOO EXPENSIVE |
| *Một, hai, ba, vô!* (mote hi ba yo) | 1, 2, 3, CHEERS! |
| *Hẹn gặp lại* (hen gap lie) | SEE YOU SOON! |

### Egg coffee

A variety of **coffee** that surprises tourists, but turns out to be creamy and delicious. Prepared with **egg yolks**, sugar, condensed milk and coffee beans.

# Typical Food

### Bánh mì

The banh mi baguette is one of the legacies of French colonialism. It is a **white bread sandwich** with pickled carrots, onions and cilantro accompanied by meat or tofu.

### Café vietnamita

Don't leave Vietnam without trying their coffee. Vietnam is the world's **largest producer** of **robusta beans**. It is **served with** a **metal filter.** Be very careful when drinking it before sleeping, Vietnamese coffee is **very strong**!

## Bun Cha

It is served with grilled
**pork** (cha) over a plate
of white **rice noodles**
(bún) and herbs with a side
of sauce.

## Goi cuon

The **Vietnamese spring roll** or
rice paper roll. It consists of pork,
shrimp, vegetables, bun (rice
noodles), and other ingredients
wrapped in rice paper.

## Pho

The **most international**
and famous **Vietnamese
dish**. It consists of a **rice
noodle soup** made with
pork broth, anise, ginger,
accompanied by beef or
chicken.

# Acknowledgements

*page*

All of these people and sites also helped make this book possible.

GRAPHIC DESIGN

Alejandra Sarmiento

— PICTURES —

Unsplash.com

iStock.com

— ICONS & DRAWINGS —

Icons by 'flaticon'

Maps by 'depositphoto'

BOOK AUTHOR

# Alberto Barambio Canet

Thank you for getting to this point and reading my Vietnam travel guide. If you enjoyed reading my book, please consider leaving a **review** on **Amazon**. Your feedback helps my **book stand out** and be found by other readers. Your support is greatly appreciated!

## Enjoy your trip to the fullest!

Alberto

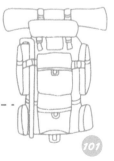

➤ LINKTR.EE/1HOURTRAVELGUIDES

🅞 @1HOURTRAVELGUIDES

Made in the USA
Las Vegas, NV
21 October 2024

10277745R00056